Twitter Fingers

A collection of tweet inspired poems and thoughts

Jasmine "Cocoa Flo" Swanagan

I can't believe I finally wrote a book y'all! It's been a long time coming and a process of mustering up the strength to share a little more of myself. Though short and sweet, this book is filled with tweet inspired poems and wisdom that really show my heart. As you read this book, I hope you see yourself somewhere between the pages, or read something that will help you along your way. I am proud to have pushed myself outside of my comfort zone and to be adding author to my list of titles.

Thank you to all of the people in my circle who have encouraged and inspired me to walk into my greatness.

As always, to God be the glory!
This is only the beginning!

I love y'all, God bless!
- Cocoa

And the tweet said...

Cocoa Flo
@thecocoaflo

Him: What that mouth do?

Me: Speak Life!

There's a tree of life in my mouth

It's roots start in my heart
limbs growing through my esophagus
producing ripe fruit that lives on my tongue

Every time I speak
seeds spew from my throat
ready to root themselves in another body
to reseed themselves in a new home

My seeds of life
plant themselves inside souls
forever producing ripe fruit on tongues
limbs growing through esophagi
roots wrapped around hearts

until there is a tree of life
in all of our mouths

Cocoa Flo
@thecocoaflo

•••

I never want to decide on a partner from a place of lack, nor do I want anybody to decide on me from that place

Hunger makes you choose some things you wouldn't choose when you're full 🍴

There is a pearl of wisdom I grew up hearing that says "you should never go grocery shopping on an empty stomach". The thought behind this wisdom is that when your stomach is empty, you are more apt to choose foods you don't need and/or foods that are less healthy. The same can be said in the dating world. Choosing a partner when you are not operating from a place of fullness will leave you accepting anything just to kill the hunger pains. Before you go shopping for partnership, check in with yourself to see if you are operating from a place of self love, and have looked after your own needs so that you are not scrounging for scraps. Be mindful. Even the bitter tastes sweet when your soul is not satisfied*.

*Proverbs 27:7

Cocoa Flo
@thecocoaflo

Processing & healing looks different for me these days because I realize you can't "busy" your way out of trauma

Trauma

always comes a knockin'

demanding my attention

asking me to look beneath the surface

I try to pacify her

give her an unhealthy habit to hold on to

hoping she will find her way out

but she's unrelenting

wants me to get to know her

to heal her

to turn a wound of a woman into wisdom

and I'm learning the sooner I listen to her

the sooner she will leave...

for now

Cocoa Flo
@thecocoaflo

At some point it stops being about the life u were born into, & becomes about the life u create. It becomes about choices. It becomes about introspection. It becomes about choosing a new way. The life u were born into is where u start but it doesn't have to be where u finish!

It's so easy to get stuck in a mindset that only choses to remember where we started. We get caught up in who we've been, who our families say we are, who society says we are, and in the trenches of trauma that cause us to be in survival mode. The trick to learning to live a fulfilling life lies in using both where you have been and who you have been as fuel to catapult you into who you are becoming!

Cocoa Flo
@thecocoaflo

•••

I love that I'm in a sweet spot when I'm so very comfortable in my skin

You are beautiful.

You don't need foundation & concealers to make up

what u think you're lacking,

Because without it,

I see the chocolate diamond you are

No need to hide in the shadow

of the shades of shadow you wear

Covering the natural shine that your eyes give

No need to contour & control the immaculately crafted creation

God has made you,

Because without it,

You're a model off the page boo,

Others will try to put down and degrade you,

But that is because they are not

You!

Girl,

You're perfectly beautiful,

Beyond beautiful,

So brilliantly beautiful,

Girl your ebony,

Is everything!

I love your brown skin!

Cocoa Flo
@thecocoaflo

Coming from poverty then making a little money is so weird cuz you have to really find the balance in managing your money so you don't squander it just cuz you got it or hoard it being afraid to lose it

When the poverty line has always been your ceiling, escaping it and beginning to make enough money to live, and thrive, can cause quite the internal confusion. Your mind wants to still operate like resources are scarce, while your pocketbook is proof that scarcity is no longer your truth. The hard part becomes mentally pressing beyond what you've always known and learning to steward your money well. It requires you find the balance. It requires you don't let the pendulum swing too far to either end of the spectrum. It requires you learn that there is value in both treating yourself to your heart's desires **AND** saving for a rainy day.

It is in the perspective shift that you learn to flourish.

Cocoa Flo
@thecocoaflo

My friend: You run your nonprofit board meetings like y'all a big organization

Me: If I run them like that now, when we become a big organization we won't be fighting to get acclimated to running correctly

They say the way you do anything
is the way you do everything.
If this is true,
I'll be running the world soon!

Cocoa Flo
@thecocoaflo

Reminder: Focus only on what you can control

At a young age perfectionism grew roots in my mind. Those roots grew me into a person who always wanted to get every single thing right. Along with the chase of perfectionism came the strong desire to hold things tight, to control, and to manipulate situations. I became a CONTROL FREAK. As I grew into womanhood, and traveled through the depths of therapy, I began to recognize perfectionism as the falsity she is and take a cloudless view of the stronghold my attempts to control had on my life. Most of my anxiety, nervousness and disappointment at any given time can be attributed to me feeling "out of control". Through practicing mindfulness, I learned to focus on the present and pay attention to what things were in my control and what things were not. Although relinquishing control is not as natural to me as I would like it to be, yet, I try to give myself the daily reminder:

Focus only on what you can control, and today that may only be your perspective.

Cocoa Flo
@thecocoaflo

Some days I forget how much light lives in me ✦

Blushing, brown, bronzed,

Luminous

Alluring

Chocolate, Cocoa, Complexion

Kind, knowledgeable, kween

Go out

Into the World

Reveal your glory

Leave light!

You can do everything right
You can follow all the rules
You can show up for all the people
But are you being authentic?
You can do it all right & still get it wrong!

- excerpt from God reading me on this
Tuesday morning 🫤🙏

It is so easy to fall into spiritual routine or even societal or cultural norms

and create a rhythm of monotony where it seems you are doing it all right.

I challenge you to periodically do a heart check.

Are you so stuck in routine that you are no longer being authentic?

Are you going through the motions?

Have you lost your grip on being present?

Check in with yourself because you can do it all "right"

and still get it wrong!

Cocoa Flo
@thecocoaflo

...

Laying here thinking

Me: I know the pandemic never ended but it's ramping back up. What are you doing leaving a secure job to walk fully into entrepreneurship?

Spirit: Trusting God.
That's what you're doing. 🙏

Life is always calling us to step out on faith.

Create the business. Write the book. Leave the job. Buy the property. DO THE THING! There will never be the perfect set of circumstances for you to leap, but staying in a place that makes you feel stagnant or less than your best self isn't ideal either. There is something so beautiful about pressing beyond the borders of your comfort zone and watching yourself walk into a new thing. We often let fear hold us back instead of allowing it to launch us into something new. Take the first step. If it doesn't work out or meet your expectations, you now have the opportunity to go back to the drawing board and a new lesson for the next jump.

Trust your gut, trust yourself, and trust the God in you.

Life is just a series of leaps and lessons.

Cocoa Flo
@thecocoaflo

•••

My friend: You used to love a project. You
stayed dating down.
Me: Girl I wouldn't call them projects. I
realized they were all just a reflection of
how I saw myself.
My friend: ...well...WOW!

Pay attention to the people you are choosing because somewhere in there you'll find some insight about how you see yourself

Cocoa Flo
@thecocoaflo

•••

Cuz the moments when I'm giving back to the next generation, to my peers, to the world, is when I realize how much my life is not my own. It's bigger than me... always 🙌

I, Cocoa,

born in an open field

raised by the beams of the sun

watered by the tears of the sky

made to be a reflection of God's beauty,

will create a garden

made of fully blossomed sunflowers

cultivated by the sound of my voice

and groomed by the imperfections of my own

petals.

#HaikusOnTwitter

Haiku is a poetic form consisting of 17
total syllables. The poem is arranged in
three lines of 5, 7, and 5 syllables

 **Cocoa Flo**
@thecocoaflo

Haiku:

You are a **temple**.
Make him kneel to worship you,
Until his knees hurt.

Cocoa Flo
@thecocoaflo

Haiku:
Airways don't function
Your love has left me breathless
Asphyxiation

Cocoa Flo
@thecocoaflo

•••

Always on the prowl
They ask me if I'm hungry
Ain't I a lion

Cocoa Flo
@thecocoaflo

· · ·

Don't believe the hype
The sky is not the limit
I relax on stars

Cocoa Flo
@thecocoaflo

•••

Haiku

Grab a life jacket.
Learn to wade in the peaceful,
Waters of your mind.

Cocoa Flo
@thecocoaflo

...

Haiku

Learn to let love fly
Do not keep it bottled up
You are capable

Cocoa Flo
@thecocoaflo

•••

Dear God,

Please give me the capacity & character to carry out all the greatness attached to my name. Make my shoulders wide enough to carry the gifts you've given me & help me not to be caught up in performing but in becoming!

Amen 🙏

There is never a shortage to the list of things we want.
We are always looking for new jobs, more money, better
partners, and more opportunities. There is absolutely nothing
wrong with wanting more, but sometimes we forget to stop and
ask if we have the capacity and character to sustain the things we
are asking for. Often we think only of getting the mansion, but
forget about the time and money it takes to maintain it. There is a
level of maturity we have to develop to not squander the
opportunities that arrive at our doorstep. In order to achieve this
level of maturity, there is a becoming process we all must go
through that builds us into stronger mental, emotional, and
moral beings. My prayer for you, and I, is that we get the desires
of our hearts, but that we also become people with strong enough
shoulders and good enough character to preserve it.

Cocoa Flo
@thecocoaflo

···

Right energy, wrong nigga

I was looking for pieces of his light in every man I met
until I discovered the flaw in expecting candles
to shine like the sun

Cocoa Flo
@thecocoaflo

···

One of the hardest things I've learned in this season is that **eliminating** people from your life doesn't have to come because they are filled with drama or they're negative or did you wrong, it could simply be because they don't fit your present or future

Learning the art of letting go can be a difficult process for most of us. It requires that we step outside of our egos, and to be honest, most of us aren't too good at that. When it comes to removing people from our lives, it's easy to think that there has to be a wrong doing or slight in order to walk away or sever a relationship. The real truth here is that it's your right and responsibility to remove anything and anyone that no longer aligns with you, your vision, your ideas, or your morals, AT ANY TIME! The sooner you master this art, the easier it becomes to allow people in, to enjoy them, to embrace experiences, and then let them go when they are no longer in alignment.

Learn to enjoy and connect with people during their season, while also remembering everybody can't go to the next level with you.

Cocoa Flo
@thecocoaflo

•••

My smile is Out of Office for the day

My smile called off today.

Say she tired of forcing her presence

Say she done stretched herself too wide for the pleasure of others

Say

these days

she is only interested in picking up shifts

when SHE feels like it.

I tell her that is fine.

There is nothing empowering about turning our body into a war zone

to appease the world!"

Cocoa Flo
@thecocoaflo

Everybody has to define what **success** looks like to them, & for me that looks like impact. It looks like kindness. It looks like giving. It looks like leading in love. It looks like blessing others. Thats's it. **Success** to me is more about who I become than what I obtain! 🙌🤍

Scene: Courtyard of Kentucky Wesleyan College (2014) a few weeks before graduation

Him: So what do you want to do with your life after graduation?
Me: I just want to be a blessing

Seven years later, on my 30th birthday, I was reminded of this conversation. As I pushed the cloud of milestone birthday anxiety aside, I relished in the simplicity of my answer. It's easy to get caught up in societies plans and projections for your life, but when I think about the sentiment, "I just want to be a blessing", it allows me to walk away from societies views and find even the most subtle ways to show up in the world. Capitalism says success looks like having a bunch of money, or fame, or resources, but honestly success looks like whatever **YOU** define it to be. Take some time and figure out what it means for you and then work on becoming your version of successful.
If you don't figure out how to outline success for yourself, the world will certainly find a way to push theirs on you.

Cocoa Flo
@thecocoaflo

•••

Boy you can like me all you want...

But where's the effort?

Liking me is cute and all

but like sir,

what am I suppose to do with that?!

Don't the good book say "like without effort is dead".... or

something like that?!

Cocoa Flo
@thecocoaflo

•••

My friends & family got me fallin apart early with the Happy Mother's Day texts/calls

I love how they always acknowledge that I've carried life in my womb & how I nurture so many other **children**/people

I was a mother the moment I saw those 2 parallel lines show up on the pregnancy test.

I was a mother the moment prenatal vitamins and ultrasounds came into play.

I was a mother the first time I heard my child's heartbeat.

I was a mother the moment I start thinking about my future and the one of my child.

I was a mother the day I decided to follow up on the spotting I was experiencing.

I was a mother the moment the doctor said they couldn't find a heartbeat.

I was still a mother in the loss.

I was still a mother in the grieving.

I am still a mother in the healing.

I am still a mother.

Cocoa Flo
@thecocoaflo

I had a disappointment happen this morning & the fact that I recognized that I could let the situation enforce the narrative that people always disappoint me or I could choose to take the moment for what it is, feel my feelings, & release, is really a testament to my **growth**

Everyday we are gifted numerous opportunities to choose whether we respond to ourselves, and others, in ways that enforce the unhealthy, wounded and survival induced thinking we have learned OR to choose a new path, to detach, to feel and release, to choose a new perspective and die to our old selves.

I hope that each time you stand at this crossroad you will choose, even in the smallest moments, to forge a new path, to shift your thoughts, to challenge yourself, to love yourself and to give yourself the grace as you grow!

Pressing through to the other side can hurt,
but baby the view is beautiful!

Cocoa Flo
@thecocoaflo

•••

"Give us this day our daily bread."

Matthew 6:11

When we pray "give us this day our daily bread" it is for more than just sustenance. We are praying for provision, for his daily salvation & for his word to be in us and breathe through us. We don't need all of it now, just a portion for this day, and he will supply tomorrow's tomorrow.

When I was a child I was taught the Lord's Prayer, but as an adult I am LEARNING the Lord's prayer.

Cocoa Flo
@thecocoaflo

•••

When your job thinks you're a slight tremor,
but they gotta find out the hard way that you're a whole ass earthquake!

I'm usually good at holding it together,
but not today,
& I'm not even sorry! 🗣️

I caused an earthquake today.

Released all this angry energy I been holding,

elevation of my voice causing seismic waves

smacking the smirk off their pale faces.

They saw the rumbling of chairs,

felt the room flooding with my wrath

as they braced for the abundance of devastation

I would surely leave behind.

They should have anticipated this catastrophe.

After all,

they've been dancing on my fault lines for awhile.

Now,

they'll remember this as the day a black woman curated a 5.0 earthquake

in NY.

I'll remember this as the day a black woman finally unleashed her feelings

left behind destruction

and DID NOT apologize!

Cocoa Flo
@thecocoaflo

•••

Black **magic** ✨

Some days
my wand doesn't work
my glitter doesn't gleam
I get my spells mixed up
say the wrong words
accidentally take care of myself
instead of everyone else

No days off for magicians
cuz when you're divine
they always expect you to perform
miracles
even when you're feeling less than miraculous

Us black girls,
learn to conjure spells early
to be the sacrifice
to save the day
abracadabra
be wind beneath everyone else's wings
be intercessor
then grow into women
turned saviors
like it's second nature
until it's instinctive

but I
done put in
too much overtime
so all I'm asking for
is a freakin day off!

Cocoa Flo
@thecocoaflo

•••

Dating really shouldn't be this hard man.
It really should be
Spend some time getting to know each
other...
Do we like each other in the present?
Are we both prepared to grow & change?
Are we both willing to give it a shot?
Alright cool! Let's see what happens

Simple.

I told myself there would be no more poems

Said I wouldn't pick up my pen to pour your praises on pages

But these half empty liquor bottles

keep confirming my conscience is now clouded.

Not sure if this will be Song of Solomon or Lamentations

love letter or goodbye note

symbol of high hope or a heavy heart.

All I know is tonight,

I can feel the magnitude of the miles marching between us,

can feel the loss of gravity's grip.

I wonder

if one morning you'll wake up,

half a calendar since the last time u saw my face,

& no longer be able to summon the scent of my skin.

If you'll forget the way my fingers feel folded against yours.

If memories & mirages of my hugs will still be enough to hold you over.

I'm praying

we never have to figure out how once aligned stars

seemed to be floating into their fault.

So let's keep the sweet smell of our love

contained in Alabaster boxes,

so on days we forget what we're fighting for

the remnants can be a shower of fresh anointing.

Distance is difficult for two delicate hearts

but here's to hoping

we can master the art of far away love

together.

#AffirmationsOnTwitter

An affirmation is a declaration of
emotional support or encouragement

Cocoa Flo
@thecocoaflo

•••

I am worthy.
I am capable.
I am not my mistakes.
I am loved.
I am more than just a survivor.
I am an overcomer.

Cocoa Flo
@thecocoaflo

•••

I am woman... Hear me roar!!

Cocoa Flo
@thecocoaflo

•••

I am a conqueror.
I am a boss in my own right.
I am genuine & kind.
I am a mountain mover.
I am intelligent.
I am resilient.
I am light.
I am an overcomer.

Who gon stop me boo? 💪🏿

Cocoa Flo
@thecocoaflo

• • •

Repeat after me:

I am worthy of love

I do not have to perform to receive love

I do not have to sell myself worthy of love

I deserve to love & be loved

I am responsible for loving me

Cocoa Flo
@thecocoaflo

· · ·

I have a gift.
I am grateful for my gift.
My gift is beautiful.
My gift does NOT look like his/her gift.
I will not compare my gift to that of
others.
My gift is not JUST for me.
I will honor my gift.
I will use my gift to help others.

Cocoa Flo
@thecocoaflo

•••

My needs are important.

I am allowed to ask for them.

It is my responsibility to ask for them.

Speaking my needs may upset other people but I am not responsible for their feelings only my own.

It is my job to uphold my boundaries when my needs are not met.

Cocoa Flo
@thecocoaflo

•••

When you change,
people will still try to call you what you
used to be

but you have to stop answering!

It's always the people who don't have access to the new version of you that want to remind you of where and who you have been. Each of us are gifted the time, grace, and the space to change, to grow and to evolve, and at it's core, that is what life is about. There are some people who will never see you beyond your past, and truthfully that's their qualm to deal with.

Don't mind them.

When they call, let the phone ring.

Cocoa Flo
@thecocoaflo

···

I clearly **miss** him today 😣

It's 12 a.m

the room is a midnight sky

the silence slowly settles in

yet sleep

won't show herself

Eyes closed,

but all I hear is his voice

all honeysuckles & harps

healing & hymnal

hoarding heavenly harmonies in his laugh

I hear how his tongue

always holds my name like a prayer

a sacred sanctuary he ain't willing to share

& my heart

begins to waltz for the only song

that seems to serenade my soul these days.

I miss the sound of him.

Cocoa Flo
@thecocoaflo

If you really like her, buy her books 🥰

What's that saying...

"If you adore her, bookstore her"

or whatever... 🧌🤍🤞🏽

Gucci, Fendi, and Dior are cool,
but have you ever had a man give you a
Barnes and Noble gift card?!

Insert swoon

Cocoa Flo
@thecocoaflo
· · ·

I live in a fairytale

I tend to live in a fairytale.

A place free of the world's constraints
where I dream of galaxies not yet crafted,
& moons so big I can reach out to touch them,
feel their power,
strong like the strides of a mother's back.

A world where I learned the beauty in being woman
before I learned my name,
then learned the beauty in being black,
in being light "through yonder window breaks".

I am the sun
magical & mindful
the world loves me
only when I don't shine so brightly.

A world where fear doesn't exist.
Every move I make is a leap of faith,
I can feel the Abraham running through my veins
I'd climb the mountaintop & sacrifice myself.

Tears drops don't even fall here,
instead they evaporate from the rims of my eyes
the universe can never find validity in my cries.
It's my world,
so happiness is the only emotion recognized.

My fairytale.
Where I am every trait I ever wanted to be,
but I'm always sad when I have to snap back to reality.

Cocoa Flo
@thecocoaflo

Disney taught me,
one day,
I would find a perfect prince,
he would slay a dragon for me,
& I would FALL madly in love

I grew up,
learned I would find a man,
human & flawed,
slaying his own inner dragons,
& I would CHOOSE to love him

We've romanticized this idea of falling in love, but to love is an active choice. I say "I love you because I choose to love you and in my choosing to look past your imperfections, love is perfected."

Cocoa Flo
@thecocoaflo

•••

black women doing anything magical, including simply existing

Me: Ain't that like a black woman ✨🙌🏿

Last night

we were just three black women

showing up to shed the weight of our week,

to leave our cares at the alter,

to conjure up ways to calm our seas.

Then,

as if on cue,

whilst standing in alignment,

we found joy,

& fellowship,

& laughter,

in each other.

& I mean ain't that just like black women

to touch & agree,

yell, "Peace Be Still",

& watch our worries lay prostrate

Cocoa Flo
@thecocoaflo

···

Replying to @thecocoaflo

My **best friend** >>> Your **best friend**

We have always been ballroom dancing
personal space has never existed
you were always the leader
while I tried to be your reflection
two stepping to the same rhythm
until I discovered how to tango in our mutualism

Simply standing behind you
feeding your ambition,
ready to lift up slumped shoulders
determined to keep your crown from slipping

While you lead the way
teaching me how to conjure up dreams
and keep one foot rooted in reality
always chief,
but I've never had a problem being Indian -
giver of adoration & patience

How sweet it is to waltz in our own symbiosis

Cocoa Flo
@thecocoaflo

···

I finally rearranged my **room** after the sexual assault I experienced & it was so freeing 🥴
I got the power over my space back 🙌🏾

When somebody steals one of your most valuable possessions, all you want to do is cling tightly to everything you have left. Your body, your senses, your mind, and even your space no longer feel like your own. Despite what some folks may believe, healing includes a process of taking back your power. For me, there were dark memories tied to the way my room was arranged. After many sleepless nights, and much deliberation, I decided it was time to make some changes to my space. The amount of liberation that came from simply rearranging the pieces was nothing short of amazing. Though I hadn't fully taken my power back in other areas, just yet, I was at least back to being the captain of my own bedroom.

I found a deeper lesson in the reorganization process; Sometimes I don't need to remove myself from the environment, sometimes I have to learn to make the environment work for me.

Cocoa Flo
@thecocoaflo

•••

I went through the fire this year
but I came out
& I didn't even smell like smoke!

Daniel 3:27

There she stood

soot falling off her clothes

gaping bullet holes in her lungs

black and blue bruises branding her body

jagged knife marks carved in her back

but did you hear me?

There she STOOD!

As she always had

resilient

with a warrior spirit

still ready to conquer the world

Cocoa Flo
@thecocoaflo

···

I feel like I got my voice back

The one area in my life I feel I have consistently struggled is with my voice. Though I am an amazing speaker, writer, and guide, sharing with people verbally has often been the hardest thing for me. I've always felt like I didn't't have anything to add to the conversation or that people didn't want to hear what I had to say. I internalized this thinking, and then taught myself to play small, to play reserved, to recluse and cower when it came to speaking up and out. It was only as I began to step out of my own confines that I realized this way of thinking was a big box of lies. **Truth is, the enemy doesn't attack any area where there is no promise.** It took me awhile to get to the point where I learned to see myself and all of the beautiful gifts I have and really embrace them. I have survived many traumatic experiences and shame has tried to turn me mute, but I learned there is no healing for me or for others in that. I've only become a survivor of life's valleys through God's grace and the use of my voice. I am thankful for the valleys for they are the places I learned to love the sound of my own voice, to scream to be heard, and to talk my talk boldly. Now that I have reached the mountain top,

I will not be silent!

Jasmine "Cocoa Flo" Swanagan is a feisty, unapologetic, and enlightened spoken word poet, author, and speaker hailing from the small city of Owensboro, KY. Cocoa holds a Bachelors in Computer Information Systems and a Masters in Health Informatics. Lyrically, she is a roaring lioness and her ability to be both down to Earth and exacting is displayed whenever she speaks. In her free time she partakes in mentoring college girls, and speaking at different schools, organizations, and workshops. Her goal is to encourage others to act, think, or heal using her own story as an example of what God, faith, and perseverance can produce. Additionally, she is the founder of Black Girl Cultivate Inc a non-profit with the purpose to mentor African American women during their collegiate journey. Follow Cocoa on all social medias

Instagram @thecocoaflo
Facebook @Cocoa Flo
Twitter @thecocoaflo

For inquiries: Email: thecocoaflo@gmail.com